EXPLORING THE ENVIRONMENT

Written by Rachel Walters

Edited by Ann Morgan

Illustrated by Ron Branagan

The Scout Association gratefully acknowledges the assistance of the Department of the Environment

Copyright © 1995
The Scout Association
Baden-Powell House, Queen's Gate, London SW7 5JS

First Edition
Printed in Great Britain by
Wednesday Press Ltd, Southend-on-Sea, Essex
Designed by Spotlight Design Services Ltd

Contents

		Page
THE BEAVER SCOUT PROGRAMME:		6
INTRODUCTION:		8
EARTH DETECTIVES:	Colony environment log	9
	Feely bags	9
	Seasonal record	9
	Pebbles and stones	10
	Mystery sounds	10
	Listen to the earth	11
	Scavenge hunt	11
	Natural patterns	11
	Ugly or beautiful?	11
	Starry night	11
	Nature detective	12
	Take a walk	12
ENVIRONMENTAL CRAFTS:	Vegetable dyes	13
	Earth printing	13
	Natural collage	13
	Environmental puzzle	13
TREES:	Splatter prints	14
	Bark and leaf rubbing	14
	Leaf printing	14
	Tree ladders	14
	Deciduous and evergreen	14
	Planting for the future	15
	Adopt a tree	15
	Tree nursery	15
	Pooters and tree beating	15
	Heart of a tree	16

		Page
BIRDS:	Feeding birds	17
	Blackbirds' dinner	17
	Build a bird table	17
	Wise old owls	18
	Kingfishers	18
	Owls and voles	18
	Nest building	18
	Hawks and sparrows	19
ANIMALS:	Where on earth?	20
	Animal pairs	20
	What animal?	20
	Animal imagination	20
	Adult and young	20
	Plan a wildlife area	20
	Country Code	21
	Animal casualty	21
	Prayer for protection	21
BAT MOBILE:		22
BALANCE OF NATURE:		
	Meal chain	24
	Woodland web of life	25
	Poison in the food chain	25
	Seals and polar bears	26
	Cat and mouse	26
	Hunting bat	26

	Page
TRACKS AND TRAILS:	
Unnatural trail	27
Tracking by smell	27
Animal tracks and signs	27
Make a footprint trap	27
Map sticks	28
Hunter and hunted	28
RARE AND ENDANGERED:	
Dead as a dodo	29
Endangered animal faces	29
Story - a whale's tale	30
Blue whale models	32
Tree map of the world	32
Save the rhino	32
FLOWERS AND INSECTS:	
Bee and butterfly walk	33
Pipe cleaner bee	33
Sowing and growing	33
From seed	33
Seeds	34
Thirsty flowers	34
Moth trap	34
Butterfly table	34
SOIL:	
Fun with fungi	35
Make a wormery	35
Footsteps of a worm	35
Make some soil	36
Soil erosion	36
Creepy-crawly experience	36
Sand cast fossils	36

	Page
RE-USING AND RECYCLING RUBBISH:	
Planting rubbish	37
Recycling relay race	37
Rhythmic rubbish	37
Recycled skittles	37
DIY recycled paper	38
Bottle piggy banks	38
Waste gobbler	39
Pollution poster	39
Litter bugs	39
APPENDIX: Scavenge hunt list	40
Blackbirds' dinner	40
KINGFISHER MODEL:	42
BLUE WHALE MODEL:	43

The Beaver Scout Programme

The Beaver Scout Programme supports and promotes the planning of balanced programmes in the Colony.

It is made up of some areas of activity and a variety of methods which take place within a framework of key principles.

The Beaver Scout Programme is illustrated on the diagram opposite and is shown as three rings, each of which is equally important.

The **Principles**, shown on the outer ring, underpin all that is done in Beaver Scouting. They describe what Beaver Scouting is all about and ensure that Colonies provide real Scouting for youngsters of Beaver Scout age.

The **Methods**, shown in the middle ring, describe how Beaver Scouts take part in the programme week by week.

The **Activity Areas**, shown in the centre of the diagram, describe what Beaver Scouts do in the programme week by week.

- Beaver Scouts learn about themselves – exploring their feelings and developing good habits of health and personal safety.
- Beaver Scouts get to know people – finding out about people in their family, the family of Scouting, the local community and the wider world.
- Beaver Scouts explore – discovering the exciting world of science, nature and technology, exploring the natural and man-made world.
- Beaver Scouts care – growing in their love of God and responding to the needs of others, the local community and the wider world.

To achieve a balanced programme, Colony Leaders are encouraged to plan at least one activity that fits into each Activity Area, at least once every three or four months. In addition, each of the methods should be used at least once during the same period.

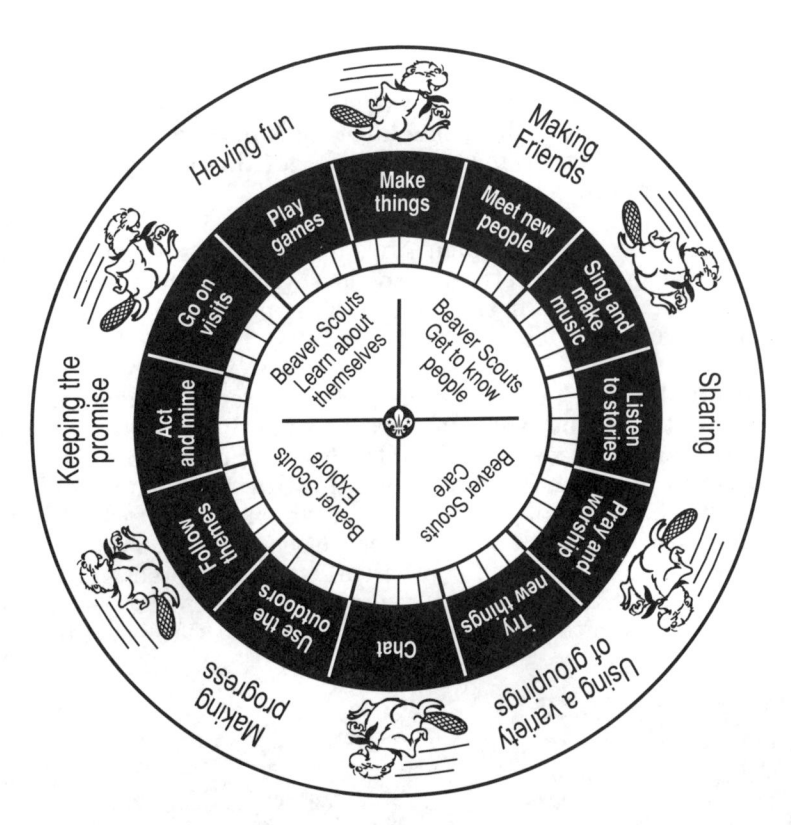

Each Activity Area can be experienced using any of the Methods. Similarly, any of the Methods can be used to introduce any Activity. Thus, the Beaver Scout Programme encourages Leaders to think of different ways to do things as well as different things to do.

Leaders are also encouraged to approach each Activity Area in a variety of ways, by including activities sometimes close to the Beaver Scouts' own experience, sometimes based in the local community and sometimes introducing them to issues in the wider world.

This booklet provides a host of activities in one or more of the Activity Areas and suggests a wide range of ways to do them drawn from the Methods in the Beaver Scout Programme.

7

Introduction

The 'Environment'

What does it mean to you? Global warming, air pollution, oil spills and ever increasing holes in the ozone layer? It is only too easy to become overwhelmed by such problems and to forget the beauty and wonder that can be found in your local environment.

So what is your local environment? In a nutshell, it's everything around you, from your home and street to the local park. It includes the water you drink, the air you breathe, all the living plants and animals, even the soil beneath your feet.

This booklet has been written to help Beaver Scout Leaders build the environment into the everyday programme of the Colony. Full of practical activity ideas, it will help Beaver Scouts to explore and understand the living world of which they are part. The booklet has been divided into a number of topic areas which can be worked through or dipped into at random as suits best. Each section contains games, crafts, activities and ideas for practical ways to protect and care for the environment and the wildlife living there. No expensive equipment is needed for any of the activities, only a willingness to get outside and start exploring.

Earth detectives

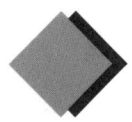

Colony environment log

To record the Colony's environmental discoveries and activities, keep an illustrated log using contributions from all the Beaver Scouts. A large scrap-book is ideal. Record things that the Beaver Scouts see outdoors or on visits. The Beaver Scouts may want to stick in pressed flowers, bark rubbings and pictures that they have drawn or prayers they have written. Remember to note down the date and where you saw things.

The local environment of every Colony will certainly be different but through participating the Beaver Scouts will have great fun wherever they meet!

Feely bags

Blindfolded, the Beaver Scouts have to identify objects in bags by feeling them. Include a variety of textures, prickly holly, damp soil, brittle twigs and perhaps a trick or two with some jelly or warm porridge!

Seasonal record

Once every few months ensure the Beaver Scouts have the opportunity to go outside to look for signs of the season. Remind them to use their senses of smell, touch, hearing, sight. Let everyone contribute something, a story, picture, word or thought which could form part of the Colony Environment Log.

AUTUMN WINTER

Pebbles and stones

Blindfolded, each Beaver Scout is handed a numbered stone. Ask each Beaver Scout to find out about his or her stone, how big it feels in the hand, its shape, any lumps and bumps? Collect the stones and with the blindfold removed, see if the Beaver Scouts can find their stones from the pile. Does the shape remind them of an animal they are familiar with and could they make up a short story about a day in the life of their stone?

Mystery sounds

Place different natural objects in a series of boxes. Egg boxes would be suitable to contain items such as stones, cones, seeds, twigs and shells. See if the Beaver Scouts can identify the contents by the sound they make when shaken. Compare the answers and tell the Colony something of interest about the objects as you pull them out.

10

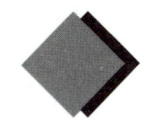

Listen to the earth
Give each Beaver Scout a supply of birdseed or sweets in a foil dish and get them to lie down and listen to the earth. Each time they hear a natural sound, for example birdsong, the creak of a branch, wind through the trees, they transfer a seed or sweet to another container. After a little while, ask the Beaver Scouts to count how many sounds they heard by counting the seeds or sweets. Talk about the different sounds and set the scene for a quiet time to say a thank you prayer for the sounds of nature.

Scavenge hunt
Prepare a list of natural objects the Beaver Scouts can find locally or photocopy the list in the back of this booklet. Organise the Beaver Scouts into groups of two or three and give each group a list and a paper bag and allow 15-20 minutes for the hunt. Allocate an adult to each group. Return to base to reveal everyone's findings!

Natural patterns
How many patterns can the Beaver Scouts find in the natural environment? Areas to explore include spiders' webs, flower petals, tree symmetry, leaf skeletons, bark rubbing, sand ripples and swirls, flames and oil and water patches. Lay a large mirror under a tree and look at the patterns the branches and clouds make.

Ugly or beautiful?
Take the Colony for a short trip outdoors and get each Beaver Scout to make a list of all the 'ugly' and 'beautiful' things they can see. These can be living or non-living. Ask older Beaver Scouts to help the younger ones. Compile the lists and place items that come up on both lists into a third column, 'different opinions'. You may want to put Beaver Scouts on the 'beautiful' list. Discuss the reasons for differences in opinion.

Starry night
On a bright, starry night take the Beaver Scouts outside to look at the stars. Stars closer to earth will look brighter than others. Can the Beaver Scouts see any shapes? Back inside, look up some constellations and make star charts by sticking foil stars onto black card. Younger Beaver Scouts could use glue and glitter to make abstract star cards.

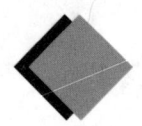

Nature detective

Borrow magnifying glasses and viewing boxes from your local school and encourage the Beaver Scouts to explore a square metre of ground. How many different things can they find?

Take a walk

An excellent way for the Beaver Scouts to learn more about the environment around them is to go on a short discovery walk. Why not invite parents along and take a picnic to eat half way? Perhaps you know someone who could point out things of environmental interest along the way. A record of the journey could be included in the Colony Log.

Environmental crafts

Vegetable dyes

Make fabric dyes from vegetables. Spinach (green), onion skins (orange) and beetroot (purple) can be cut up, boiled in a little water and strained to produce dye. The Beaver Scouts can use the dyes to paint a design directly onto a square of material or can soak pieces of knotted material to create tie dye patterns. The roots and fruits of plants can be many colours, as this activity proves. Can your Beaver Scouts name the colour that is common to them all in their leaves (green)? This is because plants only breathe using the green parts of their leaves.

Earth printing

Each Lodge can create a Colony cave painting using twigs and a pot of ink. The paintings could show some activity the Colony has undertaken recently. Swap cave paintings and see if the other Lodges can guess what the pictures represent.

Natural collage

Collect a range of natural objects such as feathers, small stones, straw, seeds, nuts, shells, moss and driftwood. Create a collage on a topic or theme by sticking the objects onto thick card.

Environmental puzzle

Let each Beaver Scout choose a picture connected with the environment from a pile of magazines. Glue the picture onto card and draw on a grid, then cut it out to make a jigsaw. Make the grid smaller for older Beaver Scouts to make the puzzle more difficult. The Beaver Scouts can swap the jigsaws with friends.

Trees

Splatter prints

Arrange different sized leaves on a sheet of paper and using a paint brush or old toothbrush splatter on paint. Remove a few of the leaves and continue using another colour. Use these to recognise the trees they come from and to consider the different outline shapes of the leaves.

Bark and leaf rubbing

Place a sheet of paper over the bark of a tree or a leaf. Rub with the flat side of a crayon or pastel. Compare the patterns made by the veins of different leaves; also the texture of bark from different trees. Ask the Beaver Scouts to select a leaf illustration to show identification of the tree.

Leaf printing

Coat the back of a leaf with washing up liquid using a brush, then apply paint over the top. Press the leaf carefully onto a sheet of paper to make a print. Experiment using leaves from different trees. Use the prints to make a collage of leaves which could reflect patterns of colours, shapes and sizes.

Tree ladders

Before the game, collect leaf specimens from different trees (and their fruit or nuts if in season) and show them to the Colony giving the names and where you found them growing. Form the Beaver Scouts into two teams sitting on the floor with their legs outstretched and feet touching. Give each pair a number. Call out a number and a tree name. The Beaver Scouts race up the ladder of legs, collect the correct specimen and run round the edge of the ladder and back to their places. Let the remainder of the Colony decide whether the correct specimen has been collected.

Deciduous and evergreen

Take a short walk to look for deciduous and evergreen trees. Explain that deciduous trees lose all their leaves in winter while evergreen trees lose a few leaves each day which are soon replaced. Can the Beaver Scouts tell the difference? Collect leaves from some of the trees and let the Beaver Scouts drip water onto them - a finger dipped into a cup works well. Leaf points allow rainwater or snow to slide off. How many different leaf shapes and number of leaf points are there?

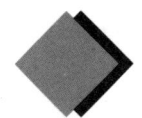

Planting for the future

If the area around your meeting place is suitable, why not plant some trees or shrubs? Each tree planted could be cared for by a different group of Beaver Scouts. Trees provide food and shelter for wildlife and help combat global warming as they absorb carbon dioxide, which is a greenhouse gas. Can your Colony find a patch of ground or a suitable tub to plant bulbs or seeds in which will also improve the environment? Photographs and sketches recording progress can be added to the Colony Log.

Adopt a tree

If you are unable to plant new trees, adopting mature trees to care for will provide a source of study for the Beaver Scouts as well as providing an ongoing link with the natural world. Try keeping a diary for each tree, recording its shape, height, diameter, bark, leaf colour changes, the life on it and its role in the environment.

Tree nursery

Go on an outing to collect tree seeds and start a Colony tree nursery. Grow seeds under cloches made from plastic drink bottles. When the trees have grown, arrange for the Beaver Scouts to give them to somebody who has space to plant them (friends, neighbours, Scout campsites). Involve a local nurseryman or gardener to help with this project.

Pooters and tree beating

Let the Beaver Scouts come face to face with a wide variety of insects by making their own pooters. Cut a short piece of clear plastic tubing (available from the brewing section of chemists) and half a drinking straw for each Beaver Scout. Place a small piece of cotton wool or fine gauze into the clear tube and insert the straw. Use the pooter to collect small insects by placing the plastic tube over them and sucking through the straw. The cotton wool will prevent the creepy crawlies being sucked up and the straws can be changed each time the pooters are used, to improve hygiene.

Spread a white sheet on the ground below a tree and shake the branch above. Let the Beaver Scouts use their pooters to look at the animal life of the tree. Remind the Beaver Scouts to handle them carefully. A couple of clear jars will allow everyone to look at particularly good finds! Nature viewers which magnify insects are a useful purchase for the Colony resources.

Heart of a tree

Spring is the best time to hear the sounds trees make as they burst back into life after a winter of leafless dormancy. Choose a deciduous tree with a diameter of at least 20cm and firmly press a stethoscope against the trunk. It may take a couple of attempts to find the heartbeat of the tree - the sound of the sap rising. The Beaver Scouts will be amazed and will want to try other trees and hear the sound their own hearts make. Perhaps a local 'tree surgeon' could assist with this activity.

Birds

Feeding birds

Let each Beaver Scout make a simple bird feeder by filling a pine cone with scraps of food and seed in lard. Hang from the branches of a tree or washing line near a window for a good view. Seed for feeding birds can be bought from garden centres and hardware stores.

Blackbirds' dinner

Most small birds eat a wide range of foods. Using the list in the appendix, the Beaver Scouts pretend to be birds and go in search of food, ticking the list if they find an example. Add up the scores to see who survived. 8-10 Well done, your sharp eyes mean you will survive. 5-7 You will be O.K. 3-4 Survival will be difficult. 0-2 Sadly you will die.

Build a bird table

With adult help, the Beaver Scouts can nail side panels onto a rectangle or square of wood (approx. 20cm x 30cm). Screw hooks into the corners and attach cord to hang. Remind the Beaver Scouts that birds should only be fed during the winter and NEVER when they are feeding their young. A shallow tray of water is also important, especially during dry and freezing spells of weather.

Wise old owls

Gather and display 10 objects collected from the environment outside the meeting place. Let the Beaver Scouts have a good look, then remove the objects and tell the Lodges that they have 5 minutes to come up with matching items. Call the Beaver Scouts back and, one at a time, pull out the objects and ask if anyone found one just the same. The members of the Lodge which has remembered and found the most items become the wise old owls for the evening.

Kingfishers

Use the master sheet at the back (page 42) of this booklet to make colourful kingfishers. Let the Beaver Scouts find a picture of some kingfishers in a book to see what colours they are. Kingfishers live along the banks of lakes and rivers where they dive into the water to catch small fish to eat.

Owls and voles

A fast and fun game to demonstrate how animals use colour to hide from predators. Prepare a number of coloured straws ranging from bright red and yellow to green, tan and black. Scatter the straws on a patch of waste land (longish grass works well). Tell the Beaver Scouts that they are hungry owls and the straws are voles. Each owl can only pick up one straw at a time and bring it back to the Leader before flying off to hunt again. If all goes smoothly, the Beaver Scouts will return the brightly coloured red and yellow straws first, the duller greens, tans and blacks coming in last. Show this to the Colony by attaching straws to a clipboard as they are returned - a little rearranging may be necessary! End with a discussion on camouflage and a hunt for camouflaged animals.

Nest building

Separate out an old bird's nest to find out what materials birds use to build their nests. What is the most common material used? During spring hang up different materials - feathers, fabric, cotton wool, string, straw - and after a period of time check the quantities to see what the birds have collected.

The Beaver Scouts can make their own nests from shredded wheat covered with melted chocolate and eggs from marzipan painted with food colouring to represent the colours of real birds' eggs.

Hawks and sparrows

Split the Colony into two teams, the 'hawks' and the 'sparrows' and allocate a home base for each. At the start of each game the teams line up facing each other. The Leader makes a statement and, if it is true, the hawks chase the sparrows. If it is false, the sparrows chase the hawks. Keep the Beaver Scouts on their toes by using a range of statements. For example 'this is a sycamore leaf' (identification), 'swans have long necks' (knowledge), 'there are clouds in the sky' (observation), 'the grass feels wet' (sensory).

Animals

Where on earth?
Design four areas, cold poles, hot desert, sky, sea. Call out the names of animals that live in these places and the Beaver Scouts must run to the correct area. On the call of 'hibernate,' the Colony must lie down as if asleep and on the call of 'migrate' form a long chain snaking around the hall.

Animal pairs
Give each Beaver Scout a card with the name or a picture of an animal on it. The Beaver Scouts have to walk around behaving and sounding like their animal until they find their mate. Collect in the cards and repeat the game.

What animal?
Pin a picture of an animal onto the back of one of the Beaver Scouts, who then has to ask questions to find out what animal it is. The rest of the Colony can only answer 'yes,' 'no' and 'sometimes.'

Animal imagination
Role playing to music can help the Beaver Scouts to appreciate the world around them by taking on the feelings of a chosen plant, animal, river or mountain. They could be otters playing at the edge of a rushing stream, mighty oak trees hundreds of years old or tiny caterpillars inching their way up the stem of a plant to feed. Become animals as a group to get the Colony into the game and then leave the Beaver Scouts to their own imaginations. Talk about the feelings the Beaver Scouts discovered.

Adult and young
Bring in pictures from books or magazines of animals and their young. Can the Beaver Scouts match the young to their parents? Glue the animal pictures, in their place, onto a map of the world and discuss the type of habitat and dangers which they face.

Plan a wildlife area
Even if your meeting place has no space to create a real wildlife area,

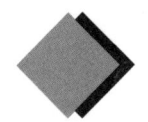

designing one on paper can be a rewarding exercise for the Beaver Scouts. Let the Beaver Scouts imagine how they could improve an area near to school or your meeting place to help wildlife. You might find it useful to discuss improvements like ponds, bird tables, wild flower areas for insects, tree planting, wet or boggy places, log piles, bird, bat or hedgehog boxes before you begin. End by discussing each others' designs and reasons for preferences expressed.

Country Code

Do the Beaver Scouts know how to take care of the countryside? The Country Code was written to help protect the plants and animals that live there. Make a wall chart to show some of the rules and encourage the Beaver Scouts to follow the code.

Here is the Country Code:
1. Enjoy the countryside and respect its life and work.
2. Guard against all risks of fire.
3. Fasten all gates.
4. Keep your dogs under close control.
5. Keep to public paths across farmland.
6. Use gates and stiles to cross fences, hedges and walls.
7. Leave livestock, crops and machinery alone.
8. Take your litter home.
9. Help to keep all water clean.
10 Protect wildlife, plants and trees.
11. Take special care on country roads.
12. Make no unnecessary noise.

Animal casualty

Each year many wild animals die on the roads. Show the Beaver Scouts the road signs that let drivers know if there are animals about (deer, toads, horses, hedgehog, cows). Can they guess what each sign means?

Prayer for protection

During a quiet time, encourage the Beaver Scouts to talk about the animals that need human care and protection for their survival. Mention these animals in a prayer at the end of the evening.

Bat mobile

Help the Beaver Scouts to make the illustrated mobile. Cut a cardboard roll in half to form the body of the bat. Colour the roll, bat and moths using pencils, crayons or paint. Use books to find the colours of real bats and moths. Cut out along the thick black lines and fold along the dotted lines. Glue the underside of area (A) and wrap the bat around the cardboard roll. Glue the tail end (B) together and do the same with the head (C). Glue on the ears (D). Attach the moths to a short length of wire with cotton and hang them below the bat. To finish the mobile, hang the bat from its back with another length of cotton.

MOTHS

BAT EARS

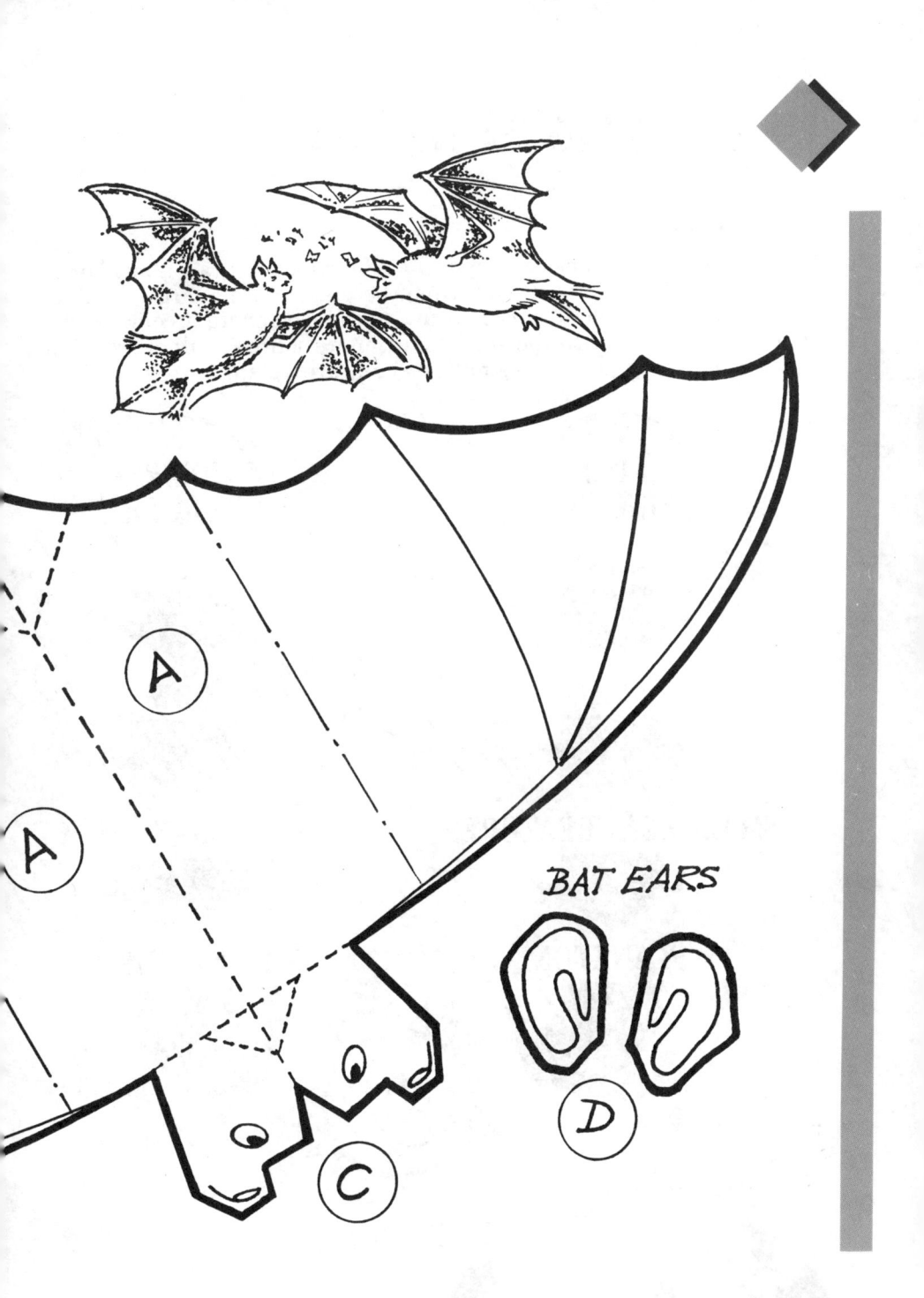

23

Balance of nature

Meal chain

Each Beaver Scout needs a paper plate on which to draw a meal or to decorate with pictures of food. Glue the plates onto a larger piece of paper and from each food item draw on the food chain it comes from, ending each time with the sun, the ultimate source of all energy. For example, fish finger - cod - small sea creature - plankton - sun.

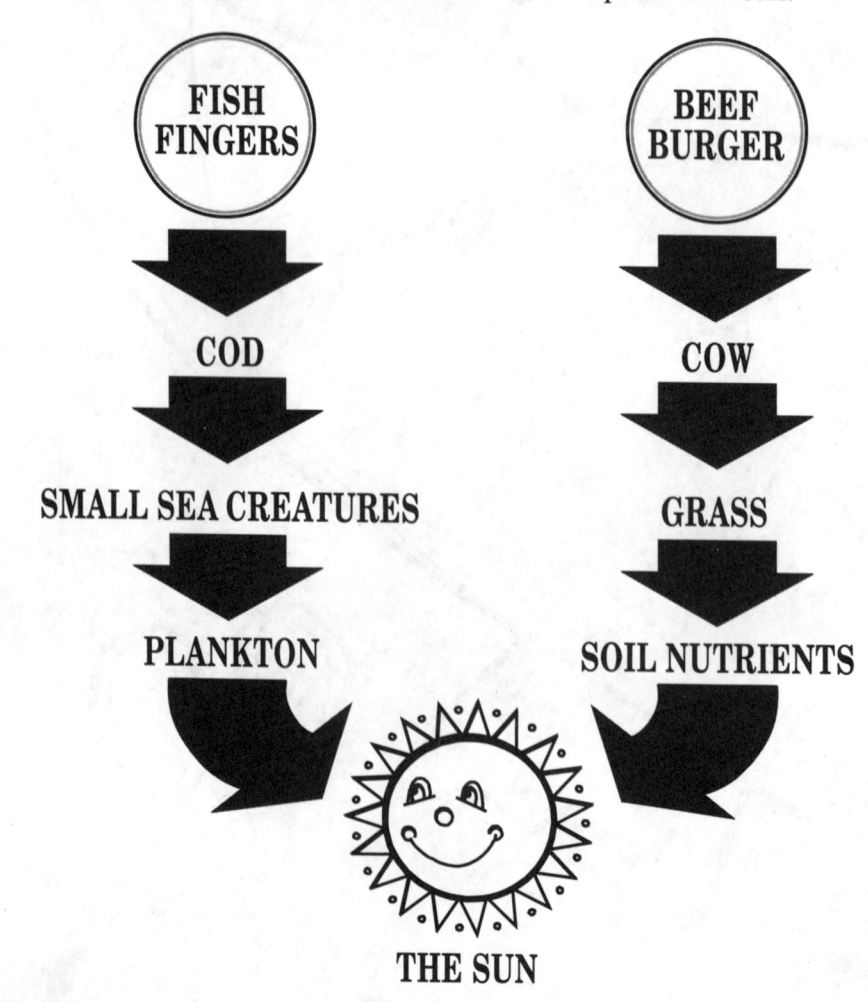

FISH FINGERS
↓
COD
↓
SMALL SEA CREATURES
↓
PLANKTON
↓

BEEF BURGER
↓
COW
↓
GRASS
↓
SOIL NUTRIENTS
↓

THE SUN

Woodland web of life

Best played at a quiet time, this game will explain to the Beaver Scouts how the natural world is connected together and that each animal and plant has an important role to play.

Form the Colony into a circle and give each Beaver Scout a card with the name or picture of a plant or animal that lives in a woodland. The Leader stands in the middle with a ball of wool and the aim is to create a food web. First, give each plant the end of a piece of wool and connect them to all the animals who eat them, and so on, until all the Beaver Scouts are connected. If you run out of woodland names, introduce other important elements such as oxygen, soil, water, sunshine or simply double some plants up. Demonstrate to the Colony how important each individual is by taking one member away. For example, the oak tree is felled and as it falls it gives a tug on the wool. Any other Beaver Scout who feels a tug has been affected by the death of the tree. Change the habitat to a seashore, river or meadow and play again.

Poison in the food chain

This demonstration tackles a difficult subject - how toxic substances become concentrated along the food chain and can eventually poison large animals and humans.

Cut out 20+ leaf shapes and tape a sweet in a wrapper to the back of each. Divide the Colony into a food chain e.g. 12 worms, 6 shrews, 1 fox. Tell the Colony that the leaves have been sprayed with a chemical poison to control pests. The droplets of poison are the sweets. The leaves fall to the ground and are eaten by worms who run and collect the leaves. Shrews eat worms so the worms must give their sweets to the shrews. In turn many shrews are eaten by one fox who ends up with a lot of poison in its body. What effect do the Colony think this might have on the fox? Poison will affect health, ability to feed and breed, survival of young or may kill the fox directly. Share out the sweets equally at the end of the game, taking great care to explain that the sweets are harmless - except to teeth - and were used to demonstrate a point. (You may decide to use another ingredient to represent 'poison.')

25

Seals and polar bears

Tell the Beaver Scouts that they are hungry seals swimming out to sea to feed. The Leader is a polar bear who stands facing the wall with newspaper fish shapes on the floor behind him. The seals have to collect as many fish as they can but must freeze if the Leader turns round. Beaver Scouts caught moving have to drop all their fish and return to the start.

Cat and mouse

Arrange the Colony to form a circle of mice. One Beaver Scout plays the cat and stands in the middle blindfolded. At a given signal one or two of the mice creep towards the cat. If the cat hears movement it points in the direction of the noise and that mouse must sit down - eaten! If a Beaver Scout manages to tag the cat they change places.

Hunting bat

Let the Colony form a circle and choose a bat who is blindfolded and stands in the circle. Choose 3 or 4 other Beaver Scouts to be moths who join the bat in the circle. Explain to the Colony that bats hunt by radar sending out electrical signals which bounce off objects and return to the bat telling it what they are. To catch the moths, the bat continually calls out 'bat' and the moths must all reply 'moth' and then it is up to the bat to catch supper!

Use the master sheet on the centre pages to make a bat mobile. Add moths that the bat feeds on to create a food chain mobile.

Tracks and trails

Unnatural trail
This game is an easy way to introduce the concept of camouflage to the Colony. Choose a short section of path (10m is ideal) around or near to the meeting place. Along the path place 10 man-made objects, some should stand out brightly like tinfoil or a shiny battery, others should blend into the background. Remember to put objects at different heights, hanging from branches, on ledges, at the base of trees or on the ground. The Beaver Scouts walk the path one at a time trying to spot as many objects as they can. They must not stop until at the end where they should whisper to a Leader how many they saw. If nobody sees all the objects, repeat the walk. End by discussing the objects and how colour and markings help animals to survive.

Tracking by smell
Prepare a trail for the Beaver Scouts to follow by rubbing fresh onion or garlic on tree trunks, walls, fences - at Beaver Scout nose height. Each Lodge has to follow the trail using their sense of smell. End with a discussion of how animals rely on their sense of smell to find food or a mate.

Animal tracks and signs
Take the Colony out in search of animal activity. Look for signs of feeding: birds leave holes and peck marks on tree trunks; squirrels, voles and rabbits strip bark leaving teeth marks; birds and mammals both leave the nibbled shells of nuts, pine cones, twigs and leaves. Record your findings with photographs or sketches done by the Beaver Scouts. These can be inserted into your Colony Log. Search for animal footprints on muddy paths, especially after rain. To preserve good footprints that the Beaver Scouts discover, place a cardboard collar round the footprint and fill with plaster of Paris mixed to a smooth paste. When dry, remove the mould and let the Beaver Scouts feel the print.

Make a footprint trap
Bury a shallow tray to the lip. Mix some of the surrounding soil with water so the resulting mixture makes a good print. Test this using a finger. Smooth off the surface and bait with a generous spoonful of

peanut butter. With a bit of luck, the next day you should find some animal tracks. Enlist the help of parents so that Beaver Scouts can try this activity at home. Ask them to bring any tracks or other findings to the next meeting.

Map sticks

Take the Beaver Scouts on a walk. Depending on the route, let them collect permissible items or tell a Leader or Helper the name of something that catches their eye. Back at base, make map sticks which reflect the route travelled. Each map stick is built up from a stick bound with pieces of wool. Each stick will be individual, reflecting the things its maker has seen, for example, green for the trees, grey for a squirrel. Objects found en route such as feathers, pine cones, dried flower heads can be incorporated.

Hunter and hunted

The Colony forms a circle, with two blindfolded Beaver Scouts standing in the middle. Ask one to name a predator and the other to name a prey it hunts for. The hunter has to catch the prey by listening, tracking and finally capturing! Stress the need for all the other Beaver Scouts to be very quiet while the game is being played. Try playing again with different numbers of prey or predators. Give the hunter a bell to carry - does this alter the method of hunting?

Rare and endangered

Dead as a dodo

Bring in some books with pictures of animals that have become extinct such as the dodo and the woolly mammoth. Do the Beaver Scouts think these animals look strange? Discover why they died out and seek the Beaver Scouts' reaction to this. Do they know which other animals are under threat? In Britain, the red squirrel, dormouse and otter and in the rest of the world, the black rhino, tiger, mountain gorilla and giant panda are all in danger of extinction. Most of these animals are becoming rare due to the disappearance of the places in which they live. Display pictures or models of these animals together with illustrations of their habitats.

Endangered animal faces

The Beaver Scouts can use face paints to paint each other's faces as different animals that are under threat - tiger, panda, rhino, mountain gorilla, kakapo, dormouse, red squirrel, otter. Some pictures on display will assist the Beaver Scouts to create a good likeness. Let each Beaver Scout tell the rest of the Colony why their chosen animal is under threat - loss of land where it lives, hunting by humans and so on.

Story - a whale's tale

Once upon a time, many years ago, a Beaver Scout Colony was meeting, just like we are tonight, when there came a loud knock at the door. In hurried the local lifeboat man, Mr. Robinson, with a very worried look on his face.

'Mr Robinson!' exclaimed Brown Beaver. 'Whatever seems to be the matter?'

'A whale has become stranded on the beach,' replied Mr. Robinson mopping his brow with a large red handkerchief. 'I need the help of the Beaver Scouts to save it. Will you help me?'

Excitedly, the Colony put on their wellies and warm coats while Brown Beaver grabbed buckets from the cupboard. Then they all made their way down the steep stony track to the beach.

Lying on the shingle was a large dark shape, steaming and blowing; it looked like a huge monster.

'Don't be scared Beaver Scouts,' called Mr. Robinson. 'Whales are very gentle animals. This whale has become stranded by mistake and needs our help.'

'I thought whales were blue,' said one of the Beaver Scouts. Brown Beaver smiled.

'No, only blue whales are blue. There are many different types of whale and they are all different colours - grey, white and black. Some are so covered in barnacles it is hard to tell what colour they are!'

Quickly, Mr Robinson explained to the Beaver Scouts that the whale needed to be kept cool and wet until high tide when the water would be deep enough to allow it to swim back out to sea where it lived. The job of the Beaver Scouts would be to splash the whale with water that Mr. Robinson and Brown Beaver would collect from the sea using the buckets they had brought. Quietly, the Beaver Scouts stood around the whale. The whale's great intelligent eyes stared back at them.

As they worked Mr. Robinson answered all the Beaver Scouts' questions. 'Do whales eat people?' 'No. Some don't even have teeth and have to sieve sea water for krill which are small fishy things, no bigger in size than your little finger. Do you fancy having some krill for your tea?' 'Yuck!'

Can whales talk?' 'Yes but not with words like we do. They use whistling and clicking sounds that can be heard by other whales many hundreds of miles away. Isn't that amazing?'

As waves started to break over the whale's giant body it gave a low drawn out rumble and slapped the shingle with its tail.

Stand well back Beaver Scouts!' called Mr Robinson. Suddenly the whale was free of the beach, turning and twisting through the water, overjoyed to be back in the ocean. Out in the bay it slowly raised its head from the water as if to get a better look at them. Then with a final flash of its tail the whale dived deep, deep down into the icy water and was gone.

'Well done Beaver Scouts!' cried Mr Robinson. 'Your hard work saved that whale. Thank you all very much.'

'Goodbye!' cried the Beaver Scouts, staring out to sea. 'Do you think it will remember us?'

'Yes,' replied Brown Beaver. 'I'm sure it will'.

Blue whale models

Using the master sheet in the back of this booklet each Beaver Scout can cut out and colour a whale. Carefully fold along the dotted line to make the whale free standing. Blue whales are on the verge of extinction with less than 10,000 individuals left.

Tree map of the world

Take a short walk and name all the trees that the Beaver Scouts can see. Draw the trees and mark where each comes from on a map of the world (a simple tree guide will give this information). Do the Beaver Scouts know where the tropical rainforests are?

On large pieces of paper let the Beaver Scouts create a tropical forest scene using pre-cut potato shapes dipped in paint. Add pictures of animals from magazines.

Save the rhino

From a stencil, each Beaver Scout cuts out a rhino. The Colony forms teams at one end of the hall. The aim of the game is to herd all the rhinos into a designated conservation area by fanning them along the floor with newspapers. Replay the game but add poachers who try to turn the rhino off course.

Flowers and insects

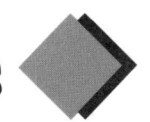

Bee and butterfly walk
Plan a short walk past areas of brightly coloured flowers. A local park, garden centre, town hall or well planted private garden (with the owner's permission) would be ideal. How many bees and butterflies can the Beaver Scouts see? Record their findings. Explore the same walk during different seasons and compare the view. Discuss how important insects are for pollinating our trees, plants and crops.

Pipe cleaner bee
Thread two beads onto the ends of two pipe cleaners. Twist to secure then twist the pipe cleaners together to form the bee's body. Glue on wings made from shiny sweet wrappers or foil. A single bee has to visit three million flowers to make one jar of honey. End the evening with some slices of bread and honey.

Sowing and growing
Grow cress or sprouting beans under different conditions to find out what factors plants need to grow. Alter the amount of water, light and temperature. Carrot tops could also be grown.

From seed
At an appropriate time of year, give each Beaver Scout some flower or vegetable seeds to germinate and care for during the growing process. A display or 'group market' could be held to view and/or sell the final results. A local charity could benefit from the produce of this activity.

Seeds

Accompanied by an adult send the Beaver Scouts out to search for seeds. This could be in the local park, along verges, in fields, gardens and woodland. Make a note of what seeds you find each month of the year and where. Experiment with the seeds to see how they travel from the parent plant to find a new place to grow. Do they float on water, stick to clothes or carry on the wind? Try germinating the seeds or store them to feed the birds during winter.

Thirsty flowers

Place a couple of flower stems (daffodils and carnations work well) or celery into a jam jar of water containing food colouring. After an hour the flower will change colour as it takes up the dye through its stem.

Moth trap

On a summer evening, a torch placed outside in a dark area will attract different flying creatures. Ask parents to join in this activity at home and to help their child identify the creatures. At the next Colony meeting the Beaver Scouts can discuss why the creatures are attracted and where they live in the daytime.

Butterfly table

Supply each Beaver Scout with a piece of cheap wood (approx. 20cm x 30cm). Screw hooks into each corner and suspend using cord. Glue a foil tray onto the table and fill with sugar solution (sugar dissolved in warm water) that will attract butterflies. Ask the Beaver Scouts to describe the colours and designs and then try to identify them from books and pictures.

Soil

Fun with fungi

Bring in some fungi or pictures from a book to show the Beaver Scouts. Be sure to point out that they are NOT edible! Create toadstools by painting yoghurt pots bright colours and adding a cardboard roll stem held in place with scrunched up paper. Place all the toadstools on the floor to make a magic circle and by candlelight tell the Beaver Scouts a story about the magic that happens in the countryside where the fungi grow. This would also be a good time for quiet thoughts or prayers.

Make a wormery

Dig up a few earthworms and place them in a plant pot of soil. Place a cylinder over the top, made from an old plastic drink bottle with the top and bottom cut off. Fill the bottle with alternate layers of different coloured soil and place some small pieces of dead leaves on the soil surface. Recreate the darkness of being below ground for the worms by covering the sides of the bottle. At the next meeting, remove the covering to see what the worms have been up to! Remember to keep the soil damp but not wet and to release the worms after a week.

Footsteps of a worm

Bring along to the meeting some earthworms in a shallow tray of soil. Let the Beaver Scouts examine them with magnifying glasses and watch how they move. Place a single worm in a tube - a kitchen roll tube is fine - and hold it to one ear. If the Beaver Scouts are quiet they will hear the scratching sound of the bristles on the earthworm's skin that it uses to move along, just like feet! Remind the Beaver Scouts that their hands will feel very warm to a worm, so handling should be kept to a minimum.

Make some soil

Bring in a tray of soil and let the Beaver Scouts investigate it. Does it smell? What does it feel like? What colours are there? Does it contain stones? Tell the Beaver Scouts that soil is made up of tiny pieces of crushed rock, air, water, dead plants and animals, and living ones. Collect quantities of these ingredients and let groups of Beaver Scouts make up their own soil. Explain that the quality and type of soil varies from region to region and this can determine the quality and range of vegetables and grain crops grown.

Soil erosion

Soil erosion by wind and water is an environmental problem, usually caused by the removal of the natural vegetation. Demonstrate this to the Colony by making two mounds of soil using a plant pot as a mould. Place moss, leaves or grass on the top of one mound. Water both together with equal quantities of water. What happens? Repeat using a hairdryer as a strong wind.

Creepy-crawly experience

Using magnifying glasses, explore the wonderful world of insects and mini-beasts. Divide the Colony into search groups to look above, below and on the ground. Place any really interesting finds in a suitable container to show to the rest of the Colony. Books and pictures displayed increase the interest and conversation.

Sand cast fossils

Pack a small box or plastic tub with clean, moist sand. Using a pencil or finger draw the swirl of a fossil into the sand. Carefully pour in the plaster of Paris. When fully set, remove and brush off the loose sand. Leave any sand embedded in the plaster for that 'just dug up' effect. This technique can be used to create a variety of fossil shapes such as leaves or bones.

Reusing and recycling rubbish

Planting rubbish
Let the Beaver Scouts bury different types of rubbish - paper, organics, plastic, metals. Label each site with the name of the item and the date. After 3-6 months dig up the rubbish. What has happened to it? Do all materials eventually decompose? Take the opportunity to invite a waste disposal expert to talk to the Beaver Scouts; invite the Cub Scouts to join in this activity.

Recycling relay race
Bring in a bag of clean rubbish for each of the Lodges. At the opposite end of the hall set up recycling points labelled 'paper', 'cardboard', 'plastic', 'metal', 'other' (glass is omitted for safety). The Beaver Scouts take it in turns to pull an item of rubbish out of the bag and run to the disposal point. It may be useful to have an adult watching out for the rubbish going into the wrong bins!

Rhythmic rubbish
Let each member of the Colony make a musical instrument from rubbish normally thrown in the bin. For example, shakers made from plastic bottles filled with peas and drums from tin cans. Ensure items are clean and all sharp edges have been removed. Bring in some lively music for the Beaver Scouts to play along to. If possible, tape the performance and play it back to the Colony.

Recycled skittles
Make up a set of pins from old plastic drink bottles, weighted with a small amount of water. The Beaver Scouts take turns to try and knock the pins over using tennis balls. What other items can the Beaver Scouts suggest that can be used for purposes other than originally intended? With parental help, ask the Beaver Scouts to bring something from home to the next meeting to prove this point.

DIY recycled paper

Soak some old newspapers in a bucket of hot water overnight. Pound the paper to pulp or liquidise it in a blender. Add three cupfuls of liquidised paper to a shallow bowl of water. Lower a piece of fine mesh metal into the bowl. Raise slowly and allow to drain. Empty onto damp material and squeeze between two boards and leave to dry. Add glitter, food colouring, pencil sharpenings and so on to create decorative papers.

Bottle piggy banks

Each Beaver Scout will need an old plastic bottle, washed and dried. With adult help, cut a slit in the back of the bottle. Cover the bottle in scraps of fabric. The bottle top becomes the pig's snout. Add eyes and a curly tail. Money saved in the piggy bank can be removed by unscrewing the bottle top. The Beaver Scouts may want to use one of the piggy banks to save money for a charity of the Colony's choice.

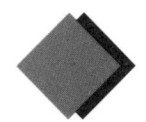

Waste gobbler

Make a waste eating monster to help keep your meeting place clean and litter free. Ask the Beaver Scouts to design their monsters on paper. Remind them that the monster will need a wide mouth to allow people to put litter in and a large tummy to hold what it has eaten. Vote to find the monster everyone likes best and encourage all the Beaver Scouts to participate in building the monster, which can stand in the hall. Alternatively, the Beaver Scouts can make their own to take home.

Pollution poster

What kind of pollution do people create in your neighbourhood? Let each Lodge tackle a different issue - car exhaust, rubbish dumping, graffiti, litter - and make an anti-pollution poster. Arrange for these to be displayed on the wall in the meeting place and at any local amenity, seeking permission if required.

Litter bugs

Take a short walk down the street and note down all the different types of rubbish the Beaver Scouts can see. Try and decide how the rubbish got there. Was it blown in the wind from somewhere else? Did somebody drop it? Remind the Beaver Scouts about the correct disposal of litter and make plans to keep their meeting place, home and school area clear of rubbish.

Appendix:

All the master sheets in the appendix can be freely photocopied for use by Members of The Scout Association.

Scavenge hunt list

Something chewed
Something perfectly straight
Something soft
Something hard
Something beautiful
A feather
Something that smells nice
A seed
A clover leaf
Something that makes a noise
Something white
Something that reminds you of yourself
Something important in nature
Something unimportant in nature
Something furry

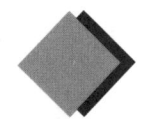

Blackbird's dinner

Here is a typical menu for a small bird. It can easily be adapted depending on the location of your meeting place.

1 snail
1 spider
1 berry
1 earthworm
2 different seeds
1 beetle
1 pine cone
1 caterpillar
1 nut
1 flying insect

Kingfisher model

Colour the Kingfisher before cutting and assembling. Cut out the body and head along the thick black lines. Glue the body around a cardboard roll, overlapping flap A. Fold along the dotted lines to make the beak. Fix the head to the body by gluing flap B to the inside of the cardboard roll making sure it matches up at the back.

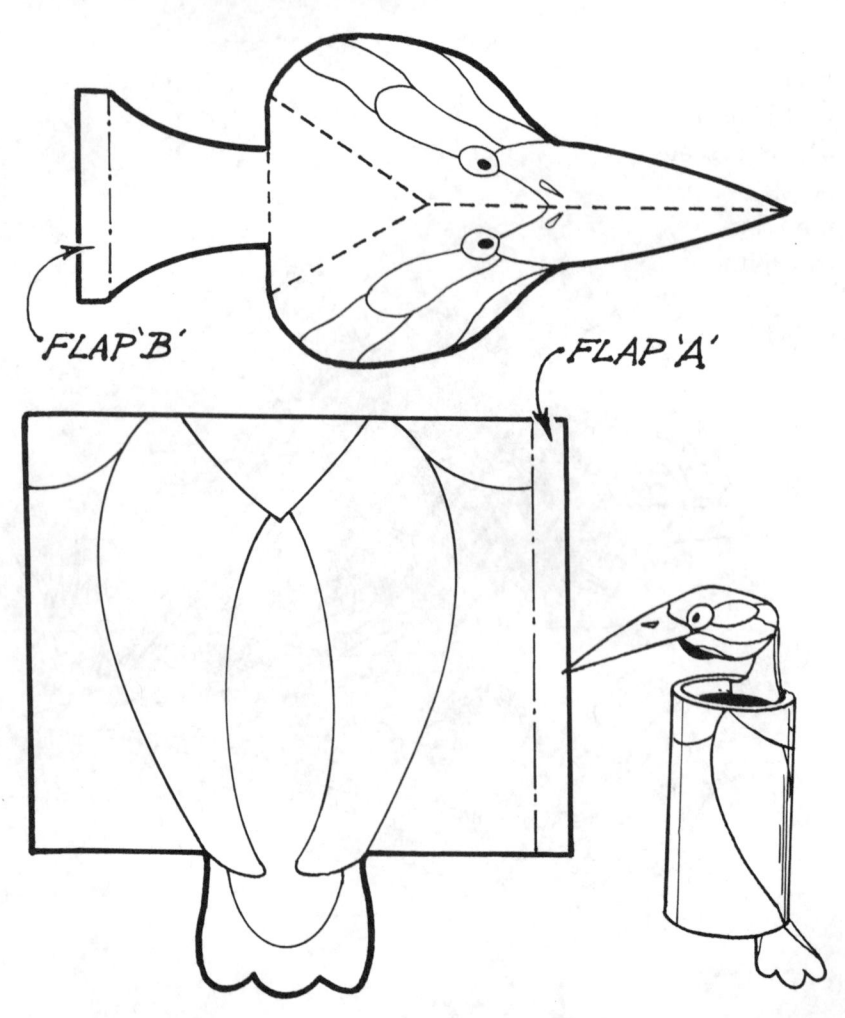

Blue whale model

Using pencils, crayons or paint, colour in the whale. Cut out the whale shape along the thick black lines. Fold carefully along the dotted lines to make your whale free-standing.

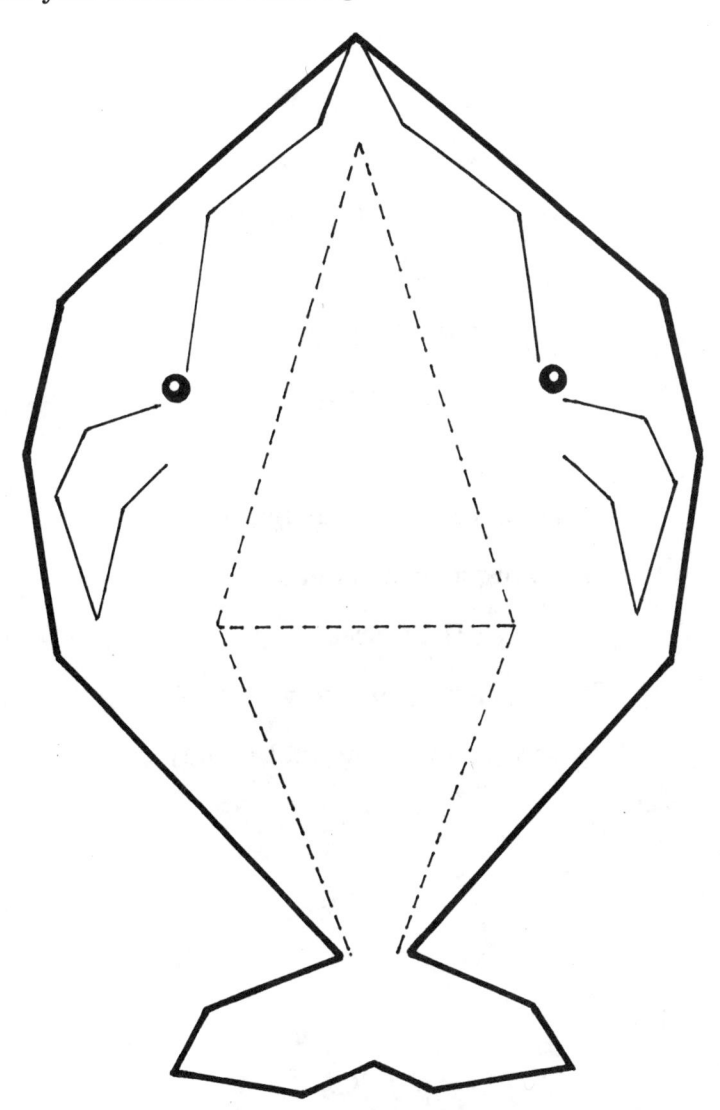

43

Booklets in this series include

Eat without heat

Everyone is special

Five minute fillers

It's a wonderful world

Let's be safe

Let's pretend

Music is fun

We promise

Exploring the environment

Looking at your community

The beaver

Exploring prayer and worship

Fun with science and technology

Notes

Notes